Mix up on the Farm

Written by Susan Frame

Illustrated by John Lund

Collins

Things are not good down on the farm.

The cow barks.

The dog moos.

Farmer Tom taps his foot.

He rubs his chin.

Tom checks the bags of food.

Quick, Tom! Quick!

Cow food for the cow.

Dog food for the dog.

The cow moos. The dog barks.

That is better!

Farmyard mix up

 After reading

Letters and Sounds: Phase 3

Word count: 55

Focus phonemes: /oo/ /oo/ /ar/ /or/ /ow/ /er/ /ee/

Common exception words: are, the, he, of

Curriculum links: Understanding the world

Early learning goals: Reading: read and understand simple sentences; use phonic knowledge to decode regular words and read them aloud accurately; read some common irregular words

Developing fluency

- Your child may enjoy hearing you read the book.
- Take turns to read a page, but encourage your child to read all the speech bubbles using animal voices. Remind them to look out for the exclamation marks on pages 9 and 13, and to read these sentences with extra emphasis.

Phonic practice

- Look together at page 4. Ask your child which word has the long /ar/ sound (*barks*). On page 6, can they find the /ar/ and /er/ sounds in one word? (*Farmer*)
- Challenge your child to read these words. Which have the long /oo/ sound like in "pool"? Which have the long /oo/ sound like in "book"?

  foot   food   moos   woof

Extending vocabulary

- Challenge your child to think of antonyms (words of the opposite meaning) to these:

  good (*bad*)   quick (*slow*)   better (*worse*)